TRUMPET 3

THE BEST OF
ESSENTIAL ELEMENTS®

FOR JAZZ ENSEMBLE

M000105977

15 ARRANGEMENTS FOR YOUNG JAZZ ENSEMBLE

ISBN - 978-1-4234-5229-4

HAL•LEONARD®
CORPORATION

7777 W. BLUEMOUND RD. P.O. BOX 13819 MILWAUKEE, WI 53213

Visit Hal Leonard Online at
www.halleonard.com

ALL OF ME

Trumpet 3

Words and Music by
SEYMOUR SIMONS and **GERALD MARKS**
Arranged by MICHAEL SWEENEY

TRUMPET

Rhythm Workout

Melody Workout

Chord/Scale Workout

Demonstration Solo

MISTER COOL

Trumpet 3

By MIKE STEINEL

TRUMPET

JA-DA

Trumpet 3

Words and Music by BOB CARLETON
Arranged by MICHAEL SWEENEY

TRUMPET

Rhythm Workout

Doo Bah Doo Bah Doo Bah Doo Bah Dit Doo Bah

Doo Bah Doo Bah Dit Dit Doo Bah Doo Bah Doo Bah Doo Bah Dit Dit Doo Bah Doo Bah

Melody Workout

Improvising On The Melody
There are many ways to change a melody to create an improvisation.

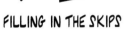CHANGING RHYTHMS

REPEATING PARTS OF THE MELODY

FILLING IN THE SKIPS

Demonstration Solo

SONG FOR SAN MIGUEL

Trumpet 3

By MIKE STEINEL

TRUMPET

SUNDAY AFTERNOON

Trumpet 3

By MIKE STEINEL

TRUMPET

Rhythm Workout

Doo Doo   Doo Doo Doo Doo   Doo Doo Doo Doo   Doo Doo Doo Doo

Doo Doo Doo Doo Doo Doo Doo Doo Dot Bah Dot Doo Doo Doo Doo Doo Doo Doo Doo Dot

Melody Workout

Scale Workout

Demonstration Solo

TAKE THE "A" TRAIN

Trumpet 3

Words and Music by
BILLY STRAYHORN
Arranged by MICHAEL SWEENEY

TRUMPET

Rhythm Workout

Melody Workout

Chord/Scale Workout

Demonstration Solo

BUBBERT'S GROOVE

Trumpet 3

By MIKE STEINEL

TRUMPET

Rhythm Workout

Doo Dot   Doo Dit   Doo Doo Bah Dot Doo Bah   Doo Dot

Doo Dit   Doo Doo Doo Doo   Doo Bah

Melody Workout

Chord/Scale Workout

Demonstration Solo

PERFIDIA

Trumpet 3

Words and Music by
ALBERTO DOMINGUEZ
Arranged by MICHAEL SWEENEY

TRUMPET

Rhythm Workout

Dit   Doo———————————   Doo Doo Doo Doo Doo   Doo Doo Doo———————

Doo Doo Doo Doo Doo   Doo Doo Doo Doo———   Doo   Doo Doo Doo Doo   Doo

Melody Workout

Chord/Scale Workout (Concert B-flat)

Demonstration Solo

BALLAD FOR A BLUE HORN

(Feature for Trumpet or Alto Sax)

TRUMPET 3

By MIKE STEINEL

TRUMPET

Rhythm Workout – (articulate lightly)

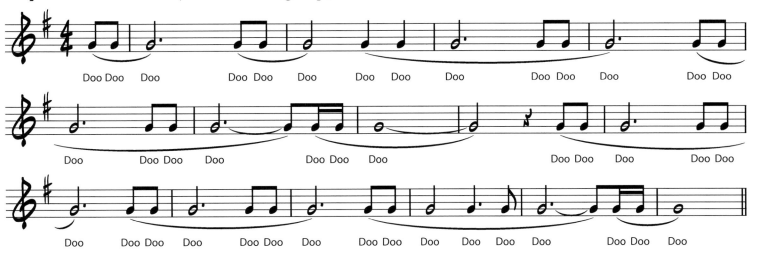

Melody Workout

Helpful Hint: Interpreting solo passages in jazz

Often we are asked to play a "solo" in a jazz piece that is not improvised but rather interpreted in a personal style ("stylized"). In these situations try to maintain the basic melody notes and focus on varying the rhythm of the written part. The demonstration solo is a good example of this technique.

Demonstration Solo – ("Stylized" treatment of melody m. 5-20)

SATIN DOLL

Trumpet 3

By **DUKE ELLINGTON**
Arranged by **MICHAEL SWEENEY**

TRUMPET

SO WHAT

Trumpet 3

By MILES DAVIS
Arranged by MICHAEL SWEENEY

TRUMPET

Rhythm Workout

Bah Doo Bah Doo Bah Doo Bah   Doo   Bah Doo Bah Doo Bah Doo Bah   Doo Bah

Melody Workout (A Guide for Improvising)

Scale Workout #1 – Concert D Dorian Scale

Scale Workout #2 – Concert E♭ Dorian Scale

Demonstration Solo

BUBBERT GOES RETRO

By MIKE STEINEL

Trumpet 3

BASIN STREET BLUES

**Words and Music by
SPENCER WILLIAMS**
Arranged by MICHAEL SWEENEY

Trumpet 3

TRUMPET

Rhythm Workout

Doo Bah Dot Doo Bah   Doo Bah Doo Bah Doo Bah

Doo Dit Doo Dit Doo Bah Doo Dit Bah   Doo Doo Bah Doo Bah Doo Bah Doo Bah Doo Bah

Doo Bah Bah Doo Bah Bah Doo Bah Bah Doo Bah Doo Bah

Melody Workout

Scale Workout

MELODY -

Demonstration Solo

ON BROADWAY

Trumpet 3

Words and Music by BARRY MANN,
CYNTHIA WEIL, MIKE STOLLER and JERRY LEIBER
Arranged by MICHAEL SWEENEY

TRUMPET

Rhythm Workout

Doo Doo Doo Doo Bah   Doo   Doo Bah   Dit   Doo   Bah

Doo Doo Doo Doo Bah   Doo   Doo Bah   Doo Doo   Doo

Melody Workout

Scale Workout

MIXOLYDIAN SCALE

"MAJOR" BLUES SCALE

Demonstration Solo

BLUES FOR A NEW DAY

By MIKE STEINEL

Trumpet 3

TRUMPET

Rhythm Workout

Bah Doo Bah Doo Doo Bah   Doo Dot   Bah Doo Bah Doo Bah

Doo Bah Doo Bah   Doo Bah   Bah Doo Dot   Bah Doo Bah Doo Bah   Doo Bah Doo Bah   Doo Dot

Melody Workout

Scale Workout

MAJOR BLUES SCALE   BLUES SCALE

Demonstration Solo

SOLO BREAK